Cambridge Discovery Readers

Starter Le

Series editor: Nich

A Little Trouble in California

By Richard MacAndrew

CAMBRIDGE
UNIVERSITY PRESS

CAMBRIDGE UNIVERSITY PRESS

Cambridge, New York, Melbourne, Madrid, Cape Town,
Singapore, São Paulo, Delhi, Tokyo, Mexico City

Cambridge University Press
c/Orense, 4 – 13°, 28020 Madrid, Spain

www.cambridge.org
Information on this title: www.cambridge.org/9788483239827

First published 2011

Richard MacAndrew has asserted his right to be identified as the Author of the Work
in accordance with the Copyright, Design and Patents Act 1988.

Printed in Spain by Villena Artes Gráficas

ISBN 978-84-8323-982-7 Paperback; legal deposit: M-25359-2011
ISBN 978-84-8323-670-3 Paperback with audio CD/CD-ROM pack for Windows,
Mac and Linux; legal deposit: M-25360-2011

No character in this work is based on any person living or dead.
Any resemblance to an actual person or situation is purely accidental.

Illustrations by Kevin Levell

Editorial management, exercises and audio recordings by hyphen S.A.

Cover design by Zoográfico

The paper that this book has been printed on is produced using an elemental
chlorine-free (ECF) process at mills registered to ISO14001 (2004), the environmental
management standard. The mills source their wood fibre from sustainably-managed
forests. No hardwood pulp is used in the production of this paper.

Contents

People in the story

Mary Lawson: a thirteen-year-old girl
Andy Lawson: a thirteen-year-old boy
David Lawson: Andy and Mary's father
Ellen Lawson: Andy and Mary's mother
Darryl: a man on the beach
Officer McMahon: a police officer

BEFORE YOU READ

. . . .

1 Look at the pictures in Chapter 1. What do you think?
    Answer the questions.

    1 The Lawson family go for a walk. Where do they go?

    ....

    2 Do they know the man there?

    ....

Places in the story

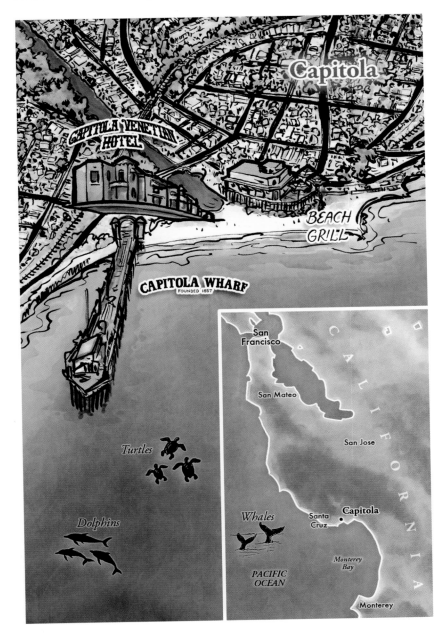

Andy and Mary's birthday

'Happy Birthday, Mary! Happy Birthday, Andy!' say David and Ellen Lawson.

'Thirteen!' says Ellen Lawson. 'You're teenagers now!'

David gives Andy his present. Ellen gives Mary her present.

'Thanks, Mum. Thanks, Dad,' say Mary and Andy.

Quickly they open their presents.

'Thank you very much!' says Mary. She looks at her new camera.

'An MP3 player!' says Andy. 'Wow! Thank you!'

Today is Andy and Mary Lawson's birthday. They are twins[1]. Andy is thirteen and Mary is thirteen too. They are on holiday with their parents in Capitola, a small town in California.

'Can we go out?' asks Mary. 'Now? I want to take some photos.'

'In a minute,' laugh her parents.

At eleven o'clock the Lawson family leave their holiday house and go to the beach. They see the funny Capitola Venetian hotel. Some rooms are red, some are green, some are yellow and some are blue. Mary takes lots of photos.

David and Ellen sit on the beach. Mary and Andy walk to the wharf [2].

A man comes out from under the wharf. He has long grey hair and a grey beard. His clothes are dirty. His face and hands look dirty too.

'He's very dirty,' thinks Mary, 'but he has friendly blue eyes.'

'Hello,' she says. 'What's your name?'

Andy looks at Mary.

'Why *is* she talking to *him*?' he thinks.

'My name's Darryl,' says the man, but he doesn't smile.

He looks at Andy, then at Mary.

'What are you doing here?' he asks.

'We're on holiday,' answers Mary. 'We're from England.'

'Well, I'm from here,' says Darryl. 'And this is *my* beach.'

Then he walks away.

'Well, that isn't very friendly,' says Mary to Andy. 'And it isn't *his* beach. It's everyone's beach.'

Then she looks under the wharf.

'What do you think?' she asks Andy. 'Does he live there? Under the wharf?'

Andy starts to say something, but then they hear their father.

'Andy! Mary!' shouts David Lawson. 'Come on! It's lunchtime.'

The teenagers run back to their parents.

'Who's that?' asks David Lawson.

Darryl is sitting under the wharf now.

'His name's Darryl,' answers Andy.

'He looks very dirty,' says Ellen.

'He is,' says Mary. 'I think he lives there. He isn't very friendly.'

'Well, don't talk to him,' says Ellen.

'But, Mum—' says Mary.

'No "buts",' says David. 'Don't talk to him again. Don't talk to strangers[3].'

LOOKING BACK

. . . .

1 Check your answers to *Before you read* on page 4.

ACTIVITIES

. . . .

2 Complete the sentences with the names in the box.

> Mary and Andy (x2)   Mary (x2)   Andy (x2)   Darryl

1 It's *Mary and Andy*'s birthday.
2 .... gets a camera.
3 .... gets an MP3 player.
4 .... go to the wharf.
5 .... has dirty clothes.
6 .... talks to a man at the wharf.
7 .... doesn't want to talk to Darryl.

3 Who do the <u>underlined</u> words refer to in these lines from the text?

1 Quickly <u>they</u> open their presents. (page 6) *Mary and Andy*
2 <u>They</u> see the funny Capitola Venetian hotel.
   (page 8) ....
3 'Why *is* she talking to him?' <u>he</u> thinks.
   (page 9) ....
4 Then <u>he</u> walks away. (page 9) ....
5 And it isn't <u>his</u> beach. (page 10) ....
6 Then <u>she</u> looks under the wharf. (page 10) ....
7 '<u>He</u> is,' says Mary. (page 11) ....

4 Underline the correct words in each sentence.

1 It's *Andy and Mary's* / *David and Ellen's* birthday.

2 Andy and Mary *go to school* / *are on holiday* in Capitola.

3 The Lawson family go to the *beach* / *wharf*.

4 The man at the wharf is very *dirty* / *friendly*.

5 Darryl *is* / *isn't* from England.

6 Darryl thinks it's *everyone's* / *his* beach.

5 Match the questions with the answers.

1 What does Darryl want to know? ☐ *d*

2 Where do the Lawson family live? ☐

3 Why does Mary think Darryl isn't friendly? ☐

4 Why do Mary and Andy leave the wharf? ☐

5 Who thinks Darryl lives under the wharf? ☐

a Because it's lunchtime.

b Mary.

c Because he stops talking to them and leaves.

d̶ What they're doing at the wharf.

e England.

LOOKING FORWARD

6 Tick (✓) what you think happens in Chapter 2.

1 Mary and Andy see Darryl on the beach. ☐

2 Mary and Andy don't see Darryl again. ☐

Chapter 2

The man with the boat

That evening the Lawson family go to the Beach Grill restaurant.

'I don't want to be here,' thinks Mary. 'I want to be on the beach.'

She finishes her food quickly.

'Can Andy and I go to the beach?' she asks. 'I want to take some more photos.'

'Isn't it too dark?' says Ellen.

'I don't know,' says Mary. 'But I can try.'

'OK,' says David. 'But don't talk to any strangers.'

'No, Dad,' says Andy. They run down to the beach.

'Come on!' says Mary.

She starts walking left, away from the wharf.

Andy starts listening to his new MP3 player.

They walk to the next beach. There are no houses and no people here.

Then they see a man and a boat. The boat is on the beach. The man is taking boxes off the boat and putting them into a white car.

Mary starts taking some photos. Andy is looking out to sea and listening to his MP3 player.

Then the man sees Mary.

'Hey! What are you doing?' he shouts.

'Nothing,' says Mary.

'You're taking photos of me,' he says and starts walking up the beach.

'I'm just taking pictures of the beach,' says Mary.
'Come here!' says the man.
'I don't like this,' Mary says to Andy. 'Come on! Run!'
But Andy doesn't hear Mary or the man.

'Andy!' shouts Mary. 'Quick! Run!'
Andy looks up and sees the man's face.
He turns and runs fast after Mary.

The man stops and watches them. Then he goes back to the boat and his boxes.

Mary and Andy run.

They see someone in front of them. It's Darryl.

'Hey!' he shouts. 'Where are you going? Come here!'

'Don't stop!' says Andy.

They run away from Darryl and back to the house.

'Don't say anything to Mum and Dad,' Mary tells Andy.

'OK,' answers Andy.

They go into the house.

'Hi, Mum! Hi, Dad!' they say.

'It's time for bed,' says David.

'But, Dad—' starts Mary.

'No "buts",' says Ellen.

In their bedroom, Mary says, 'I want to go back to that beach tomorrow.'

'Oh no!' thinks Andy. But he doesn't say anything.

Chapter 3

Officer McMahon calls

'Are we going to Seaworld today?' asks Andy at breakfast the next morning.

'No,' answers his mother. 'We're going out on a boat today. In Monterey Bay.'

'Are we going to see some whales?' asks Mary. 'Or some dolphins?'

'How about turtles?' asks Andy. 'Turtles are my favourite!'

David and Ellen Lawson leave the table.

Mary starts looking at the photos on her camera. Andy looks too. They can see the man and the boxes and his car.

'These photos are very dark,' says Mary.

'What's that man doing?' asks Andy.

She gives Andy the camera.

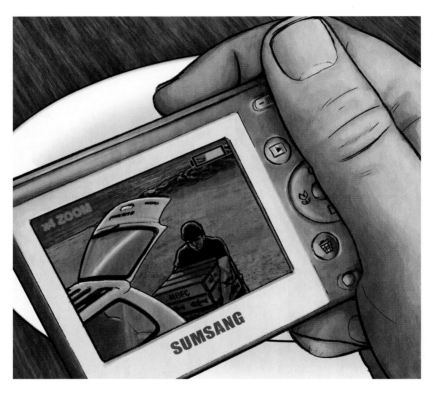

'What's in those boxes?' he says. He can see some letters on the boxes – MBFC – and he can see a picture on the man's arm. It's a bird[4] – an eagle.

Just then they hear someone at the door.

Ellen goes to the door and opens it. A police officer is standing there.

'Can I help you?' she asks.

'I'm Officer McMahon,' says the police officer. 'Capitola Police.'

David goes to the door too.

Andy and Mary can hear the police officer, but they can't see him. Mary looks at Andy. He puts the camera behind him.

'He can't be here about the photos,' says Mary to Andy.

'How can we help you, Officer?' asks David.

'The blue car across the street,' says Officer McMahon. 'Is that yours? It's in front of ...'

Mary smiles at Andy and he brings out the camera.

'No,' says David. 'Our car's red.'

'Oh! That's OK then,' says Officer McMahon. Then he looks into the kitchen and sees Mary and Andy. He turns to David.

'Where are you from?' he asks, a strange look on his face.

'England,' replies David. 'We're on holiday. We're here for ten days.'

'OK,' says Officer McMahon. 'Good.'

Then he turns and leaves. Ellen Lawson closes the door. She looks at David.

'Good?' she asks. 'Why is it "good"?'

'Strange man,' says David.

LOOKING BACK

1 Check your answers to *Looking forward* on page 13.

ACTIVITIES

2 Underline the correct words in each sentence.

1 The Lawson family eat at the *Beach Grill restaurant* / *beach*.
2 Andy and Mary see a man putting boxes into a *car* / *boat*.
3 Mary and Andy *tell* / *don't tell* their parents about Darryl and the man on the beach.
4 Mary and Andy look at photos of *Darryl* / *the man on the beach*.
5 There *is a bird* / *are some letters* on the man's arm.
6 Officer McMahon wants to know about the *red* / *blue* car.
7 Officer McMahon *sees* / *doesn't see* Andy and Mary at their holiday house.

3 Put the sentences in order.

1 Mary and Andy see Darryl in front of them. ☐
2 Officer McMahon talks to David and Ellen about their car. ☐
3 Mary wants to take some more photos on the beach. ☐*1*
4 A police officer comes to the holiday house. ☐
5 Andy and Mary see a man, a boat and a white car on the beach. ☐
6 Mary and Andy look at photos on Mary's camera. ☐

4 Are the sentences true (*T*) or false (*F*)?

1 Mary doesn't want to be at the restaurant. ☐T

2 The man on the beach sees Andy taking photos. ☐

3 A woman goes to the Lawson family's holiday house. ☐

4 The Lawson family are going to Sea-World. ☐

5 Mary wants to go to the beach again. ☐

6 Andy can see a picture of a bird on the boxes in the photos. ☐

7 The Lawson family's car is red. ☐

8 Andy and Mary speak to Officer McMahon. ☐

5 Answer the questions.

1 What is the man doing on the beach?

....

2 Who does Mary take photos of?

....

3 What is on the boxes?

....

4 Why does Andy put the camera behind him?

....

LOOKING FORWARD

6 Tick (✓) what you think happens in the next two chapters.

1 Andy and Mary talk to their parents about Darryl and the man in the photos. ☐

2 Andy and Mary see what is in the boxes. ☐

Chapter 4

Where does the white car go?

In the afternoon the Lawsons go out on a boat and see some whales and turtles. In the evening they go back to their house.

'I love turtles,' says Andy. 'Do you know – they swim over eleven thousand kilometres to get here?'

'And some people eat them,' laughs Mary.

'Mary!' says Ellen. 'Stop it!'

Andy laughs too.

'Come on,' says Andy to his sister. 'I want to go to the beach again.'

'OK,' says Mary.

'Come back in half an hour,' says Ellen.

'OK, Mum,' says Andy.

On the beach Mary sees a white car drive by.

'That's the car!' says Mary. 'It's that man again. Come on!'

She starts running.

'Mary! Stop!' says Andy.

But he starts running too.

The car drives away and turns right. Andy and Mary run after the car. The car turns left.

Andy stops running.

'He's in a car, Mary,' he says. 'And we're not.'

'Don't stop,' says Mary. 'Come on!'

They run up the street and turn left. And then they stop. They can't see the car.

They look up and down the street, but there's no white car. They start to walk back. Mary looks sad.

'I'm going to look down here,' she says and turns right. Andy waits for her. Then he hears her.

'It's here,' shouts Mary.

Andy runs to his sister. The white car is there – it's in front of a grey building.

There is a door in the front of the building. It's open. Mary looks left and right. There's no one on the street at this time of the evening. She runs to the door. Andy runs after her.

They look into the building. It's just one big dark room. With the door open, they can see a little. There are boxes everywhere.

'Listen,' says Andy. They can hear noises. Strange noises. The noises are coming from the boxes. There's a man at the back of the room. They can hear him, but they can't see him. He's speaking on the phone.

Mary takes Andy's hand.

'Quick!' she says. They run into the building and sit behind some boxes.

'OK,' says the man. 'Tomorrow evening ... Good ... Seven o'clock ... Bye.'

Then they hear the man leave. The door closes. The room goes dark. They hear the car drive away.

In the dark, Andy finds the door. He tries to open it, but he can't.

'We can't get out,' he says.

Chapter 5

Getting away

'Help!' shouts Mary.

Andy shouts too, but then he stops.

'No one can hear,' he says. 'There's nobody here at this time of night.'

Mary's face is sad.

'I'm sorry,' she says.

'Why?' asks Andy.

'We're here because of me,' says Mary. 'I'm sorry.'

'It's OK,' says Andy. But he thinks, 'No, it isn't.'

They wait. After about five minutes they start to see in the dark.

Andy looks at the boxes.

'Look,' he says 'MBFC. These are the boxes in your photo.'

'There's something in these boxes,' says Mary. She can see a small foot. 'They're ... turtles!'

'Oh no!' says Andy. 'Turtles are beautiful! Why are people taking turtles from the sea?'

'For food?' asks Mary.

Andy looks at Mary. This time she isn't laughing.

'Someone is selling these turtles,' says Mary. 'That's why they're in boxes.'

'People can't do that,' says Andy. 'It's wrong. We must tell the police.'

'Yes, and we must get out,' says Mary. 'That man's going to come back.'

Andy goes to the back of the room.

'There's a window here,' he says to Mary. 'We can get out, but it isn't going to be easy. Come on. Help me.'

He takes a box and puts it under the window. Mary takes a box too and puts it next to Andy's.

After two minutes they have six boxes under the window. Andy gets on to the sixth box and opens the window. He looks out. There's a tall tree next to the building.

'Come on,' he says to Mary.

He helps her up.

Then Andy gets out of the window and over to the tree. He helps Mary out of the window too.

Just then, they hear a noise and look down. There's someone below them in the street.

LOOKING BACK

1 Check your answers to *Looking forward* on page 25.

ACTIVITIES

2 <u>Underline</u> the correct words in each sentence.

1 Andy likes <u>*turtles*</u> / *whales* very much.
2 *Andy* / *Mary* says people eat turtles.
3 *Andy* / *Mary* sees the man in the white car.
4 The white car turns *right and then left* / *left and then right*.
5 There are lots of *men* / *boxes* in the grey building.
6 Mary and Andy *hear* / *see* the man in the room.
7 Mary's got a photo of *the room* / *boxes* on her camera.
8 Andy sees a *door* / *window* at the back of the room.

3 Answer the questions.

In Chapters 4 and 5, who ...

1 goes to the beach again? *Andy and Mary*
2 is speaking on the phone in the building? ....
3 can't open the door of the big dark room? ....
4 sees the letters MBFC on the boxes? ....
5 thinks someone is selling turtles? ....
6 thinks the man is going to come back into the building?

....

7 says it isn't going to be easy to leave the building?

....

4 Put the sentences in order.

1 The white car is in front of a grey building. ☐
2 The man gets into the car and drives away. ☐
3 Andy wants to go to the beach. ☐1☐
4 Mary and Andy put six boxes under the window. ☐
5 Andy and Mary hear someone speaking on the phone. ☐
6 Mary sees the white car by the beach. ☐
7 Mary and Andy go into a big dark room and sit behind some boxes. ☐
8 Andy helps Mary get out of the building. ☐

5 Answer the questions.

1 What do Andy and Mary see in the boxes?

....

2 What does Andy want to tell the police?

....

3 Who do Mary and Andy see under the tree?

....

LOOKING FORWARD

● ●

6 Tick (✓) what you think happens in the next two chapters.

1 Darryl waits for Andy and Mary in the street. ☐
2 Darryl takes the turtles. ☐
3 Mary and Andy tell Officer McMahon about the turtles. ☐

Chapter 6

Who is taking the turtles?

'Oh no!' says Andy. 'It's Darryl.'

'Why is he here?' asks Mary.

Darryl puts a hand up.

'Take my hand,' he says.

Andy looks at Mary.

'We mustn't talk to him,' he says.

Mary says nothing.

'Come on,' says Darryl.

He takes something out of his jacket. It is a police ID card.

'I'm a police officer,' says Darryl. 'A detective[5].'

'Then you don't live under the wharf,' says Mary.

'No,' laughs Darryl and he helps the teenagers down.

'Your parents are looking for you,' says Darryl. 'The police too.'

'We're looking for the police,' says Mary. 'We want to tell them about the turtles.'

'What turtles are you talking about?' asks Darryl quickly.

Andy and Mary tell Darryl about the boxes and the man in the building.

'Someone is taking turtles from Monterey Bay and selling them.' says Darryl. 'I want to speak to that man in the building.'

'Mary's got a photo of him on the beach!' says Andy.

'Yes!' says Mary. 'But it's very dark ...'

'I want to see that photo too,' says Darryl. 'But first we must find your parents.'

They start walking.

Darryl and the two teenagers turn onto Monterey Road. David and Ellen Lawson are talking to Officer McMahon in front of their house.

Andy and Mary run to their parents.

'Andy! Mary!' says Ellen Lawson. 'Are you OK?'

Ellen puts her arms round her children. Then she sees Darryl.

'What are you doing with him?' she asks.

'We're OK,' starts Mary, 'And Darryl—'

'Why are you late?' asks Officer McMahon.

Andy looks at the police officer. Then he sees his left arm.

'It's you,' says Andy.

'What are you talking about?' says Officer McMahon.

'This is the man, Darryl,' says Andy. 'Mary's photo isn't very good, but you can see the bird on the man's arm. Look at it. This police officer is taking the turtles!'

43

Darryl walks quickly over to Officer McMahon and takes his arm.

'I don't understand,' says Officer McMahon. 'I'm not—'

'You're coming with me,' says Darryl and he takes out a phone.

Ellen Lawson's mouth is open.

'It's OK, Mum,' says Andy. 'Darryl's a detective.'

'People are taking turtles from the sea and selling them,' says Mary, 'and Darryl is looking for those people.'

There is the noise of a police car not far away.

'I've got some questions for you,' says Darryl to Officer McMahon.

David Lawson looks at Mary and Andy.

'And I've got some questions for you,' he says.

Darryl puts a hand on David Lawson's arm.

'Don't be angry with them,' he says. 'They're detectives too. Good detectives.'

LOOKING BACK

1 Check your answers to *Looking forward* on page 39.

ACTIVITIES

2 Put the sentences in order.
1 Darryl says he is a detective. ☐
2 Andy sees a bird on Officer McMahon's arm. ☐
3 Andy sees Darryl under the tree. ☑1
4 Andy knows who is taking the turtles. ☐
5 Andy and Mary tell Darryl about the turtles. ☐
6 David Lawson is angry with Mary and Andy. ☐
7 Mary and Andy tell their parents about Darryl and the turtles. ☐
8 Darryl takes Andy and Mary to their parents. ☐

3 Match the questions with the answers.
1 What has Darryl got? ☑e
2 What does Darryl want to see? ☐
3 Who is waiting for Mary and Andy at the holiday house? ☐
4 How does Andy know about Officer McMahon? ☐
5 Who's got a photo of the man with a bird on his arm? ☐

a David and Ellen Lawson and Officer McMahon.
b The photo of the man on the beach.
c There's a bird on his arm.
d Mary.
e̶ A police ID card.

4 Are the sentences true (*T*) or false (*F*)?

1 Darryl is waiting for Mary and Andy in the street. ☐ T
2 Darryl is a detective. ☐
3 Darryl lives under the wharf. ☐
4 Darryl knows about the boxes and the man with the boat. ☐
5 Mary's photo is dark. ☐
6 Mary's got a photo of Darryl. ☐
7 Ellen Lawson knows Officer McMahon is taking the turtles. ☐

5 Underline the correct words in each sentence.

1 Darryl *is* / *isn't* a police officer.
2 Darryl *helps* / *doesn't help* Andy and Mary down from the tree.
3 *Officer McMahon* / *Darryl* has a picture of bird on his arm.
4 *Darryl* / *Officer* McMahon is taking the turtles.
5 *Mary and Andy talk to* / *Darryl talks to* Ellen Lawson about the turtles.
6 *David and Ellen think* / *Darryl thinks* Mary and Andy are good detectives.

6 Answer the questions.

1 What is Darryl's job?

....

2 Why does Darryl want to talk to Officer McMahon?

....

3 Who is the man in Mary's photo?

....

Glossary

[1]**twin** (page 7) *noun*   a person who has a brother or sister born on the same day

[2]**wharf** (page 8) *noun*   boats stop here

[3]**stranger** (page 11) *noun*   someone you do not know

[4]**bird** (page 20) *noun*   an animal that flies

[5]**detective** (page 41) *noun*   a kind of police officer